A Note to Parents

DK READERS is a compelling program for beginning readers, designed in conjunction with leading literacy experts, including Dr. Linda Gambrell, Distinguished Professor of Education at Clemson University. Dr. Gambrell has served as President of the National Reading Conference, the College Reading Association, and the International Reading Association.

Beautiful illustrations and superb full-color photographs combine with engaging, easy-to-read stories and informational texts to offer a fresh approach to each subject in the series. Each DK READER is guaranteed to capture a child's interest while developing his or her reading skills, general knowledge, and love of reading.

The five levels of DK READERS are aimed at different reading abilities, enabling you to choose the books that are exactly right for your child:

Pre-level 1: Learning to read
Level 1: Beginning to read
Level 2: Beginning to read alone
Level 3: Reading alone
Level 4: Proficient readers

The "normal" age at which a child begins to read can be anywhere from three to eight years old. Adult participation through the lower levels is very helpful for providing encouragement, discussing storylines, and sounding out unfamiliar words.

No matter which level you select, you can be sure that you are helping your child learn to read, then read to learn!

LONDON, NEW YORK, MUNICH,
MELBOURNE, AND DELHI

For Dorling Kindersley
Senior Editor Laura Gilbert
Managing Art Editor Ron Stobbart
Publishing Manager Catherine Saunders
Art Director Lisa Lanzarini
Associate Publisher Simon Beecroft
Category Publisher Alex Allan
Production Editor Siu Yin Chan
Production Controller Rita Sinha
Reading Consultant Dr. Linda Gambrell

For Lucasfilm
Executive Editor J. W. Rinzler
Art Director Troy Alders
Keeper of the Holocron Leland Chee
Director of Publishing Carol Roeder

Designer Lisa Sodeau
Editor Lindsay Kent

First published in the United States in 2011
by DK Publishing
375 Hudson Street, New York, New York 10014
11 12 13 14 15 10 9 8 7 6 5 4 3 2 1
Copyright © 2011 Lucasfilm Ltd and ™
All rights reserved. Used under authorization.
Page design copyright © 2011 Dorling Kinderley Limited
177105—04/11

DK books are available at special discounts when purchased in bulk
for sales promotions, premiums, fund-raising, or educational use.
For details, contact:
DK Publishing Special Markets
375 Hudson Street
New York, New York 10014
SpecialSales@dk.com

A catalog record for this book is available
from the Library of Congress.

ISBN: 978-0-7566-8263-7 (Paperback)
ISBN: 978-0-7566-8262-0 (Hardcover)

Reproduced by Media Development
and Printing Ltd., UK
Printed and bound in China by L. Rex Printing Co., Ltd

Discover more at
www.dk.com
www.starwars.com

Contents

4   What is a duel?

6   Weapons

8   Jedi training

10   Sith methods

12   A forgotten menace

14   Duels on Naboo

16   Conflict on Kamino

18   Battle of Geonosis

22   Rescuing Palpatine

24   Battle of Utapau

28   A Sith Lord revealed

30   Close contest

34   Master and apprentice

38   Death Star duel

40   Cloud City clash

42   Battle of wits

44   Final confrontation

48   Glossary

DK READERS

PROFICIENT READERS

4

STAR WARS
Ultimate Duels

Written by Lindsay Kent

What is a duel?

A duel is a battle between two people. Opponents might use weapons, such as a lightsaber or blaster, or they may not use weapons at all. The Jedi are trained in the ways of the Force and are skillful fighters. They have fought many duels with warriors, often with those known as the Sith—the only opponents with the powers and skills to match the Jedi.

Master Yoda
Yoda is an ancient Jedi. He can sense a disturbance in the Force due to the return of the Sith, but he doesn't know which one is the new Sith Lord.

The Sith are trained in the dark side of the Force but were thought to be extinct. The Sith are far from extinct. They are in hiding, waiting for the right moment to return and wreak revenge on the Jedi. With the return of their old enemy, the Jedi have many more duels to fight!

Jedi Knight Luke Skywalker fights Sith Lord Darth Vader in an epic battle.

Sith Lord
Darth Sidious is the new powerful Sith Lord. For years he manages to keep his Sith identity secret by pretending to be a politician.

A lightsaber can easily cut through durasteel blast doors.

Crystal
A crystal is placed inside the handle of each lightsaber. The crystal focuses the energy released from a power cell and the blade of energy is produced.

Weapons

The most common weapon used by a Jedi in a duel is a lightsaber. A lightsaber is an elegant weapon. The user must be well-trained in the ways of the Force in order to wield it skillfully in combat. Every lightsaber is made to suit the owner's needs and preferences. It is held like a sword, but instead of a metal blade, a lightsaber has a beam of energy that bursts from the handle when the weapon is ignited.

Crystal placed inside

Lightsaber handle

A lightsaber can cut through most things, but not the blade of another lightsaber. The weapon is used like a sword in combat, but a lightsaber can have other important uses. Jedi can use the Force to predict incoming energy bolts from blaster guns and use a lightsaber to deflect the bolts back toward their opponent.

Colorful
The color and length of a lightsaber's energy blade depends on the type of crystal that has been used to make the weapon. Crystals from the planet Ilum produce either a green or a blue lightsaber blade.

A Sith apprentice called Darth Maul favors a double-bladed lightsaber, as it suits his style of combat.

Jedi training

At one with the Force
Even during battle and situations of extreme stress, a Jedi tries to remain calm and focused.

The Jedi Order is an ancient peacekeeping organization. The Jedi use the Force to defend and to protect others, so it is important that they learn to fight skillfully in a duel. It takes years to become a Jedi so training usually begins at a very early age. Younglings are taught to use lightsabers. At times their eyes are covered while they train so they can learn to feel the Force and use their instincts, instead of relying on what they can see.

Trainees also learn how to use the Force to move objects without physically touching them. A Force pull enables Jedi to bring something to them. A Force push is a powerful technique that can repel objects or opponents.

Jedi Master Qui-Gon Jinn performs a Force push to repel several droids.

A Jedi novice learns to live by the Jedi Code—a set of rules the Jedi obey. According to the Code, the Jedi must use the Force for good. They should have compassion for all life, and must engage in combat only in defense of others or themselves.

Fighting fit
Jedi Knights are experts in using lightsabers but they must also be physically strong and fit. Yoda teaches a young Jedi, named Luke Skywalker, to be agile.

Sith methods

Like the Jedi, the Sith are able to sense and use the Force when they duel. The Sith's Force training, however, varies greatly from that of the Jedi. They use the dark side of the Force and gain their power from raw emotions, such as anger, pain, and hatred. The Sith do not value life or feel compassion, and their ferocious style of combat reflects their attitudes.

The Sith act in aggression and not in defense, and feel free to do anything in battle—no matter how devious.

The Sith can use the Force to produce Force lightning. They channel the Force through their bodies and discharge powerful bolts of energy from their palms and fingertips into their opponents. The Sith can also use the Force to choke a victim without actually touching them.

Ferocious
The Sith use anger in battle. Their rage can make them extremely powerful.

A Sith Lord named Darth Vader often uses the Force choke on opponents.

A forgotten menace

The Jedi first meet their old enemy, the Sith, on a planet called Tatooine. Jedi Master Qui-Gon Jinn is escorting Queen Amidala to Coruscant when a Sith named Darth Maul arrives on a speeder bike, and begins a fierce attack on Qui-Gon. The mysterious assailant fights with a double-bladed lightsaber. It is clear that he is highly trained in the ways of the Force. He battles the Jedi Master with incredible skill and power.

Qui-Gon struggles to cope with Maul's surprising skills and only narrowly escapes when Queen Amidala's starship picks him up. The Jedi is unprepared for the encounter because the Sith were believed to be extinct. It is clear from this duel that the Sith are very much alive and more powerful than ever.

Qui-Gon Jinn
Qui-Gon Jinn is an experienced Jedi Master. He was taught by a Jedi called Count Dooku.

A new Sith
Darth Maul is Darth Sidious' apprentice. His entire body is covered in tattoos revealing his origins as a Nightbrother of Dathomir.

Duels on Naboo

Obi-Wan Kenobi

Obi-Wan is a skilled and dedicated Jedi. When he cuts Darth Maul in half, he becomes the first Jedi in centuries to defeat a Sith in battle.

Qui-Gon Jinn and his apprentice, Obi-Wan Kenobi, encounter Darth Maul again on Naboo. Maul fights both Jedi at once until Obi-Wan becomes separated from Qui-Gon and the Sith. Qui-Gon is no match for Maul and he is fatally injured. Obi-Wan is upset and angry, and his raw emotions take him toward the dark side of the Force for a time, but he manages to calm himself.

As Obi-Wan and Maul fight, it is clear that the Sith is more powerful. Maul uses the Force to push Obi-Wan over the edge of a pit, leaving the Jedi hanging from a pipe. Darth Maul believes victory will be his and smiles and taunts his opponent. He kicks Obi-Wan's lightsaber into the pit, but the Jedi uses the Force to retrieve Qui-Gon's weapon. In a surprise move, Obi-Wan jumps out of the pit and strikes Maul with one swift blow.

Arrogance
Darth Maul is over-confident and so he underestimates Obi-Wan. This leads to his downfall.

Conflict on Kamino

Clone Army
The clones are exact copies of Jango Fett but they grow much faster than a normal human. This allows the Kaminoans to produce thousands of soldiers in a short time.

Obi-Wan travels to a water planet called Kamino where he discovers that the Kaminoans have been creating a huge clone army. The army was supposedly ordered by a Jedi called Sifo-Dyas, but Obi-Wan learns that the Jedi Council doesn't know about the army. Every soldier is a copy of a bounty hunter called Jango Fett.

When Obi-Wan meets Jango, the bounty hunter tries to escape, and he and Obi-Wan begin a violent brawl.

Jango can't use the Force, but his suit contains many gadgets, and these give him an advantage when Obi-Wan loses his lightsaber.

Jango binds Obi-Wan's hands together with his wrist-mounted wire and Obi-Wan falls over the edge of a landing platform. Jango is dragged down, too, but just in time he manages to cut the wire and escapes on his starship *Slave I*.

Jango Fett
Jango Fett is one of the most successful bounty hunters in the galaxy. His special suit is fitted with weapons such as wrist blades and blaster pistols. It also has a jetpack.

Anakin Skywalker
Anakin is one of the most gifted Jedi to ever live. He was a slave before he joined the Jedi Order and became Obi-Wan's apprentice.

Darth Tyranus
Count Dooku is lured to the dark side of the Force by Darth Sidious. Dooku becomes the Sith Lord's apprentice, Darth Tyranus.

Battle of Geonosis

On the rocky planet of Geonosis the Jedi must fight another Sith opponent. Jedi Knight Obi-Wan Kenobi and his Padawan, Anakin Skywalker, discover that a once-respected Jedi, Count Dooku, has turned to the dark side. Obi-Wan and Anakin must stop Dooku from escaping.

Obi-Wan tells Anakin to wait, but the young Padawan is impatient. With his lightsaber ignited, he rushes toward Dooku who uses Force lightning to throw him against a wall. Obi-Wan and Dooku begin to duel with lightsabers and Obi-Wan is injured. Dooku is about to kill Obi-Wan when Anakin stops him. Anakin tries to defeat the Sith Lord, but Dooku overpowers him and slices off Anakin's right arm. With both Jedi wounded, the Sith is victorious.

Classic weapon
Count Dooku's lightsaber has a curved handle that is shaped to fit his hand. This gives him extra control of the weapon in his chosen fighting style.

Obi-Wan and Anakin lie injured in Dooku's secret hangar when another Jedi enters—Master Yoda. Count Dooku uses Force power to hurl objects at Yoda, and causes sections of the ceiling to fall on him. Yoda defends himself, diverting the missiles away by using his own Force powers. Yoda and Dooku then fight with lightsabers. In spite of his age Yoda shows amazing athletic abilities.

Special spaceship
Count Dooku's spaceship has a solar sail. When it is unfurled, the sail opens ahead of the ship, collecting energy particles from space that are used as fuel.

Dooku is unable to defeat Yoda, and is in danger of being captured. Dooku distracts him by endangering Obi-Wan and Anakin. He uses the Force to drop an enormous pillar toward the injured pair. Dooku knows Yoda will need all of his power to save them, so he is able to slip away in his Solar Sailer.

Rescuing Palpatine

When the Trade Federation appears to kidnap Chancellor Palpatine, Jedi Knights Obi-Wan and Anakin are sent to rescue him. Once again they must face their old foe, Count Dooku. Obi-Wan is knocked unconscious with a powerful Force push by the Sith, but this time Anakin isn't so easy to overpower.

Devious Chancellor Palpatine pretends that he has been kidnapped. He wants Dooku and Anakin to fight so that Anakin can defeat Dooku and become Palpatine's new apprentice.

Count Dooku throws Obi-Wan across the room with a Force push.

Dooku goads Anakin during their fight. He believes he still has the advantage, but he is suddenly outmaneuvered by Anakin, who severs both of Dooku's hands. Unable to fight, Dooku falls to his knees before Anakin. On Palpatine's command, Anakin kills Dooku.

Dishonorable
Killing someone who is hurt and weak is not the Jedi way. Anakin's decision to kill Dooku takes him much closer to the dark side—just as Palpatine hopes it will.

Sinkhole city
The planet of Utapau is covered in deep holes, known as sinkholes. The Utapaun people have built cities in these holes.

Battle of Utapau

After the failed attempt to kidnap Chancellor Palpatine, the Jedi Council sends Obi-Wan on a mission to hunt down General Grievous. Palpatine believes that the Clone Wars cannot end until Grievous is captured. Obi-Wan travels to Utapau where he finds Grievous in one of the planet's large sinkhole cities.

Grievous is part-living creature and part-droid, which makes him a difficult opponent to beat.

He has four artificial arms, which enable him to wield four lightsabers at once with brute force and speed.

Although Grievous has been trained in lightsaber combat he cannot use the Force like Obi-Wan. The Jedi is able to anticipate Grievous' blows and cuts off several of the cyborg's hands, forcing him to flee.

General Grievous
Grievous was one of the greatest military leaders on the planet of Kalee until he was fatally injured in a shuttle crash. He was then rebuilt as a cyborg.

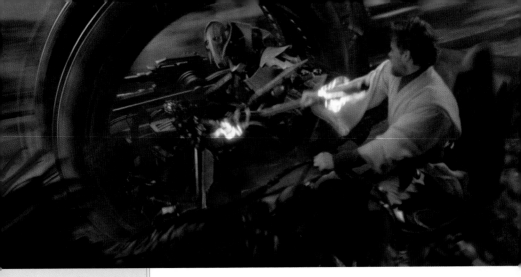

Varactyls
Utapau is home to giant bird-like lizards called varactyls. The creatures are used for transport as they are agile and have huge claws so they can grip the stone sides of the sinkholes.

Grievous escapes on his wheel bike, pursued by Obi-Wan on a varactyl named Boga. Obi-Wan loses his lightsaber during the chase, but manages to grab Grievous' electrostaff and the duel continues. The cyborg has the advantage because he is very strong and has an armored body, and Obi-Wan is nearly beaten. The Jedi is knocked over the edge of a landing platform and hangs precariously above a vast chasm.

Just as Grievous approaches, armed with his electrostaff, Obi-Wan uses the Force to grab Grievous' pistol and blasts his opponent. Normally the plates that protect Grievous' internal organs would have deflected the blast, but during the brawl Obi-Wan had managed to loosen the plates, so the shot kills the General.

Deadly weapon
Grievous' guards use weapons called electrostaffs. They are made of a very strong material that does not break even after being struck by a lightsaber blade. Each end of a staff emits deadly levels of energy.

A Sith Lord revealed

When Chancellor Palpatine's true identity as a Sith Lord is revealed to Anakin, Jedi Master Mace Windu goes to the Senate to arrest him. Mace is accompanied by three other Jedi, but they are caught off-guard when the Chancellor suddenly ignites a lightsaber and attacks them. Within seconds he kills everyone except Windu.

The Jedi Master and Palpatine engage in a fierce lightsaber duel. Windu manages to disarm Palpatine, but the Sith uses the dark side to bombard Windu with Force lightning.

Windu deflects the lightning back toward Palpatine with his lightsaber, causing Palpatine's face to become scarred. Windu is about to finish off Palpatine when Anakin steps in and cuts off Windu's hand that was holding his lightsaber. Palpatine seizes the opportunity to attack Windu, using more Force lightning to throw the Jedi through the window to his death.

Scarred
In a speech to the Senate, Palpatine lies about the cause of his scarred face. He says it happened when the Jedi tried to assassinate him as part of a Jedi plot against the Republic.

Palpatine is a terrifying opponent.

Close contest

As Supreme Chancellor Palpatine becomes more powerful within the Republic, the Jedi are in grave danger. Palpatine commands the Clone Army to carry out Order 66—exterminate the Jedi. Most Jedi are killed, but Yoda survives. He then goes to the Senate to face Darth Sidious.

Sidious uses Force lightning to throw Yoda across his office. It appears that he is too strong for the Jedi Master, who lies motionless. The Sith Lord gloats about his apparent victory, but Yoda surprises him with a powerful Force push.

Royal Guards
Sidious' Royal Guards are well-trained, but they are no match for Yoda. The Jedi defeats them using the Force with just a small movement of his hands.

Yoda and Sidious begin a frenzied lightsaber duel and the two highly skilled Masters are evenly matched. Still fighting, they mount the Senate speaking platform that begins to rise, lifting the two opponents into the Senate Chamber.

Emperor's podium
The ceiling of Palpatine's office opens up and the speaking platform rises into the Senate Chamber. Standing on the podium, Palpatine declares himself to be Emperor.

Senate Chamber
The chamber is the largest room in the Senate Building on Coruscant. Within the chamber are thousands of pods. Each pod holds Senators from all over the galaxy.

Both Yoda and Sidious are powerful, and as their lightsaber duel continues in the Senate Chamber, it is clear that neither is able to defeat the other easily. Sidious uses the Force to launch huge Senate pods at Yoda, which causes the Jedi to drop his lightsaber. Yoda gains the upper hand when he pushes a pod back at Sidious, who falls. However, the Sith is able to grab hold of a pod and clambers to safety.

Sidious uses brutal Force lightning again and Yoda deflects it back, but the counterblow throws him over the edge of the pod and down to the chamber floor. Yoda is not badly hurt, but he realizes that he cannot defeat Sidious this time and decides to flee.

Escape
Yoda escapes thanks to Bail Organa who picks him up in his airspeeder. Yoda then travels to a planet called Dagobah where he hides from the Emperor for many years.

Evenly matched
Vader and Obi-Wan try to Force push each other, and they are both repelled across the chamber.

Master and apprentice

It is with sorrow that Obi-Wan learns that Anakin has succumbed to the dark side of the Force. He has become Sidious' new apprentice and is now called Darth Vader. Obi-Wan goes to the volcano planet of Mustafar to confront his old apprentice, and finds Vader in a lava mining facility. Obi-Wan tries to reason with Vader, but it is clear that he has lost his friend to Sidious.

Vader and Obi-Wan ignite their lightsabers and begin an intense battle. Vader is consumed with rage and hatred, and the duel is brutal. During the fight the shields protecting the mining facility from the lava are shut down, and the entire structure begins to melt into a river of molten lava. With Obi-Wan on a lava skiff and Vader on a droid, the former friends continue their fight, hovering above the lava.

Sadness
Obi-Wan is distraught at having to fight his apprentice and friend. Anakin had been like a brother to him.

Flaming rivers
Lava rivers flow all over Mustafar. The lava bursts from beneath the planet's surface like huge fiery fountains. The skies above Mustafar are always dark because they are filled with black clouds of ash and smoke.

As Obi-Wan and Vader approach a riverbank, Obi-Wan manages to jump off the lava skiff onto a high slope. He sees that Vader is about to do the same, and warns him not to, as he has the higher ground. Vader is arrogant and doesn't listen. He leaps toward Obi-Wan, allowing the Jedi Master to perform a final winning blow, and Vader is defeated.

Obi-Wan cannot bring himself to kill his former comrade, however, and so he leaves him there. Darth Sidious senses Vader's plight and flies to Mustafar where he finds his new apprentice barely alive. He then uses his dark powers to save him. Medical droids reconstruct Vader's body using robotic parts and encase the Sith in a black suit that allows him to breathe.

The Emperor and Darth Vader are a fearsome pair. The Emperor has complete control over the Galactic Empire. With Vader by his side, there is no one with the courage or the ability to challenge him.

Reconstruction
Medical droids use advanced technology to rebuild Darth Vader's body. There is little left of the man who was once Anakin Skywalker. Vader is now more machine than man.

Death Star duel

On the Imperial Death Star, Obi-Wan Kenobi and Darth Vader meet again after many years. Since the Emperor seized power, Obi-Wan has been in hiding, living a simple, solitary life, but all that is about to change. A member of the Rebel Alliance named Princess Leia is captured by Imperial troops and asks for Obi-Wan's help.

Death Star
The Death Star is a huge space station, built by the Emperor. The Death Star has a weapon that is so powerful it can destroy an entire planet.

Darth Vader immediately senses Obi-Wan's presence on the Death Star and goes to face him. They fight with lightsabers as before, but the duel is very different from their last encounter. Obi-Wan is older and weaker, and sees that Vader is too strong for him. But beating his former apprentice is not part of his plan. Obi-Wan knows that if he sacrifices himself he will become one with the Force and more powerful, so he allows Vader to kill him.

Force Ghost
After death, some Jedi, like Obi-Wan Kenobi, are able to use the Force to talk to the living and advise them. These Jedi are called Force Ghosts.

Cloud City clash

The duel on Cloud City is
between Darth Vader and a young
Jedi-in-training named Luke
Skywalker. Before Luke can
complete his training with Yoda, he
rushes to Cloud City on Bespin,
sensing that his friends Princess
Leia, Han Solo, and Chewbacca are
in danger. He doesn't realize that
his friends' capture is part of a plan
hatched by Vader to bring Luke
to him.

Luke doesn't have enough
experience to face Vader, and
throughout the battle Vader
uses his superior Force powers
and lightsaber skills against him.

Vader's attack is relentless and in a final blow, he severs Luke's hand. Vader then reveals that he is Luke's father and tempts him with the power of the dark side. But Luke chooses to sacrifice himself rather than be corrupted and falls down a shaft. He is sucked into a chute, however, and ends up clinging to the underside of Cloud City until Princess Leia rescues him.

Father and son Vader and the Emperor find out that Luke is the son of Anakin Skywalker— Vader's former self. Luke will be a powerful addition to the dark side if they can turn him.

Cunning plan
Luke's Jedi powers have grown strong and he has become wiser. When Luke confronts Jabba, he lets Jabba capture him—it is all part of his plan.

Jabba the Hutt
Jabba is a notorious crime lord, who lives on a desert planet called Tatooine. His legless body looks like a giant slug.

Battle of wits

Crime lord Jabba the Hutt has captured Luke Skywalker's friends Princess Leia, Han Solo, and Chewbacca, so Luke must free them. He goes to Jabba's palace and demands their release, but Jabba just laughs at him. Jabba doesn't physically fight Luke—he has his own methods! He opens a trapdoor and Luke falls into the rancor's den. The rancor creature is huge and ferocious, but Luke manages to defeat it.

Jabba then orders his guards to feed Luke and his friends to the Sarlacc. Jabba eagerly awaits Luke's death, but he doesn't know that Luke has hidden his lightsaber in his droid, R2-D2, who is on Jabba's sail barge.

The terrifying rancor is a huge reptile-like creature.

R2-D2 ejects the lightsaber toward Luke who then destroys Jabba's men. Thanks to the chaos Luke causes, the guards on Jabba's barge are distracted, giving Leia the chance to strangle Jabba. In the battle of wits between Luke and Jabba, the Jedi proves wiser.

The Sarlacc
Hidden beneath the desert sands of Tatooine is a creature called the Sarlacc. Its mouth is surrounded by tentacles that capture its prey.

Explosive!
Luke and his friends escape just as Jabba's sail barge explodes.

A trap
The Rebel Alliance obtains plans showing how to shut down the Death Star's defense shield, so it can be destroyed. They don't realize that the Death Star is already operational and extremely dangerous.

Final confrontation

The battle between Luke and the Emperor on the Death Star begins with words, not physical combat. When Luke arrives, the Emperor tries to tempt him to join the dark side. The Emperor tells Luke that it is his destiny and encourages Luke to give in to his anger and fight him. For a while Luke refuses to be provoked, but the Emperor senses how much Luke's Rebel friends mean to him and uses this to goad him.

The Emperor reveals that he knows that the Rebels plan to attack the Death Star and that he allowed false information about the Death Star to reach Rebel hands. The Emperor tells Luke that his Rebel friends are about to be destroyed; Luke cannot hold back his rage any longer. Luke sees his lightsaber next to the Emperor and draws it to him. He tries to strike the Emperor, but Vader stops him. Father and son then begin their final battle.

Over-confident When Vader arrives with Luke, the Emperor sends his guards away. The Sith Lord believes that he is invincible and they will not be needed.

The Sith defeated

It appears that seeing Luke revives the former Jedi within Vader. When he decides to stop the Emperor, he turns away from the dark side of the Force.

Luke's anger and experience make him stronger than the last time he fought Vader. Now Luke has the upper hand and the opportunity to end Vader's life. Although he is tempted to kill Vader, Luke manages to control his rage. He refuses to kill his father and be turned to the dark side. Instead he throws down his lightsaber and surrenders.

The Emperor is surprised by Luke's strength of mind, but is furious that he will not join him. Enraged, the Emperor bombards Luke with Force lightning in a one-sided battle, clearly enjoying the pain he is causing Luke.

As Luke writhes in agony he begs his father to help him, but Vader looks on and does nothing. The Emperor is about to end the young Jedi's life, when Vader suddenly picks up his evil Master and throws him down a reactor shaft, killing him. By doing this he saves his son and destroys the Empire.

A machine no more
Vader has gone and Anakin Skywalker has returned, but because the Emperor's Force lightning has wounded him and damaged his suit, he cannot survive for long. His last wish is to see Luke through his own eyes.

The Emperor falls to his death.

Glossary

Agile
Quick and well-coordinated.

Anticipate
To know that something will happen before it takes place.

Apprentice
A trainee or learner.

Arrogant
Believing that you are better than others.

Assassinate
To kill a ruler or politician.

Bounty hunter
Someone who searches for and captures people for a reward.

Brute force
Physical power.

Chasm
A deep hole.

Clone
An exact copy of something or someone.

Clone Wars
The conflict between the Republic and the Separatists, who want to destroy the Republic.

Compassion
To feel sympathy for someone.

Consumed
To be taken over by something.

Counterblow
A blow given in return during a fight.

Cyborg
Someone who is part-living matter and part-robot.

Deflects
Blocks something that is coming toward you and forces it back toward an opponent during battle.

Devious
Dishonest and sly.

Disarm
To take a weapon away from someone.

Diverting
Changing the direction of something.

Elegant
Something that is graceful and refined.

Exterminate
To totally destroy something.

Extinct
Something that has died out.

Force
The energy created by all living things.

Goad
To anger and irritate someone.

Gloats
Is smug about something.

Loyalty
Being devoted to something or someone.

Opponents
People who fight against each other in a duel.

Outmaneuvered
When a person is beaten or outdone during a fight.

Padawan
A trainee Jedi who is being instructed by a Jedi Master.

Particles
Tiny pieces of something.

Podium
A raised platform for a public speaker.

Precariously
Dangerously.

Provoked
To have angered someone.

Rancor
A large and deadly reptile-like creature.

Rebel Alliance
A group of people who want to remove the Emperor from power.

Repel
To force something back.

Skiff
A small boat-like airspeeder.

Taunts
Makes fun of someone.

Technique
A particular way of doing something.

Trade Federation
A group of merchants and transporters who control the movement of goods in the galaxy.

Underestimates
Doesn't value someone's abilities highly enough.

Unfurled
Something that has been spread out.

Wield
To handle a weapon or tool with ease.